# DRIVING THE
# OLD SPANISH TRAIL
## THROUGH UTAH AND ARIZONA

*Ruth Friesen* & *Steven Heath*

Published by the Old Spanish Trail Association
www.oldspanishtrail.org

*Traveling the Old Spanish Trail Through Utah and Arizona*

Ruth Friesen & Steven Heath

**Disclaimer**
While considerable effort has been made to ensure that information herein is
accurate at the time of publication, errors and omissions may have occurred, and road
conditions and signage may change over time. Maps published in this guide are for
reference only and are not to be used for navigation. The authors, the Old Spanish
Trail Association, and others involved in producing this guide book disclaim any
liability to any party for any errors or omissions in this guide or for any injuries or
losses incurred while using this guide book or any potential travel disruption that
occurs while traveling the route.

Cover and book design by Ruth Friesen
Photos © Ruth Friesen
Cover photo © Bernice Payne, Metal artist Eldon Holmes of Cleveland, Utah
Back cover photo of Green River © Col. Al Matheson
Horseshoe Bend photo © Christopher K. Eaton Photography,
        www.terra.photography.
Maps © Interpretive Design, LLC. Overall route map courtesy National Park Ser-
vice National Trails Intermountain Regional Office

Printed and bound in the United States of America
First Edition
First printing November 2015
ISBN: 978-0-9967873-0-7
Library of Congress: 2015915845

Published by the Old Spanish Trail Association, Albuquerque, New Mexico
www.oldspanishtrail.org
Made possible by a grant from the Grand Staircase Escalante Partners, Kanab, Utah
http://gsenm.org

*Dedicated to*
*generations of trail scholars*
*and trail travelers,*
*historic and new*

# How to Use this Guide

## Road Maps

This guide is intended to be used in conjunction with a state highway map or atlas. Maps provided in this text are sketches for orientation purposes and do not provide detailed road information. Some atlases, such as the Delorme Atlas and Gazetteer, indicate where the Old Spanish Trail was, but the exact location may be disputed by trail scholars.

**Milepost markers** are very helpful for travelers driving federal and major state highways. On south-north trending highways, the convention is to start at 0 on the south end of the route and at every mile place a marker. For example, on I-15 the Utah/Arizona border is mile 0 and as you travel north the numbers increase to milepost 134 as it exits onto I-70. West-east trending roads begin at 0 on the west end and increase as one drives eastward. On I-70 it is 0 at its junction with I-15 and as it heads eastward, Richfield is at mile 40 and the Colorado border is roughly milepost 233. This guide uses the notation MP ###. **GPS coordinates** are provided when finding a location might be challenging.

## Names of Old Spanish Trail Routes

This guide uses the Old Spanish Trail names in accordance with the National Park Service labeling. See the map on the following pages. Some Trail scholars call the Northern Route the Main Route.

# CONTENTS

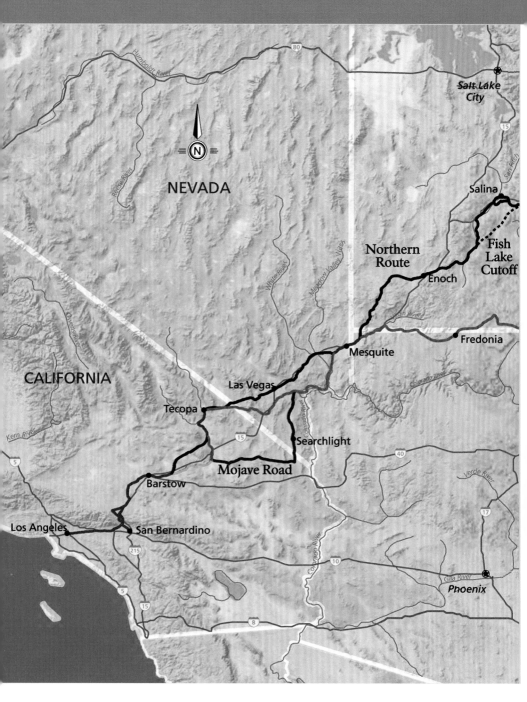

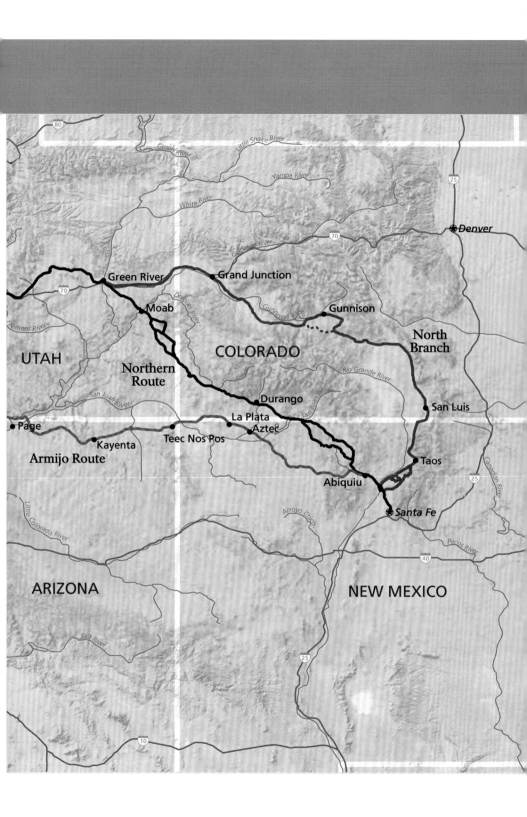

# A BRIEF HISTORY OF THE OLD SPANISH TRAIL THROUGH UTAH AND ARIZONA

The Old Spanish Trail, which was recognized by Congress as a National Historic Trail in 2002, was an overland trade trail between Santa Fe, the provincial capital of New Mexico, and the Mexican pueblo of Los Angeles. The trail and its various branches followed earlier routes established by American Indians. A glance at the official trail map shows that modern roads and highways follow the historic route closely, since passage through the canyons and across the rivers of Utah and Arizona left, then as now, few options.

With the settlement of California by the Spanish at the end of the 18th century, there was a great need of woolen goods for its settlers. This condition still existed in 1821 when Mexico declared its independence from Spain. A combination of explorations by Padres Dominguez and Escalante in 1776 from New Mexico into Colorado and Utah back to Santa Fe; Francisco Garces from the Tucson, Arizona, area to Los Angeles by way of present-day Needles, California, also in 1776; and explorer Jedediah Smith from Salina Canyon, Utah, to Needles in 1826, opened what became known as the Old Spanish Trail.

The story of trade between New Mexico and California began in 1829 when 25-year-old Antonio Armijo received authorization from José Antonio Chavez, New Mexico Minister of Interior and Foreign Relations, to lead a trade caravan from Santa Fe to California. Armijo gained the services of 60 men including muleteers and assembled a pack train loaded with woven woolen goods, primarily serapes and blankets, products of New Mexico's sheep industry. Armijo and his backers hoped to trade these goods for California mules and horses which were in abundance at the California rancheros. The official report of Armijo's trade journey, along with Armijo's diary, was dispatched by Minister Chavez to Mexico City on May 14, 1830, and was published in the *Registro Oficial de Gobierno de los Estados Unidos Mexicanos* on June 19, 1830.

They followed a path that approximated the current boundary between Utah and Arizona. They forded the Colorado River at the site known as the Crossing of the Fathers in honor of the 1776 Dominguez-Escalante expedition.

The route that Armijo and his men traveled was quickly determined to be too difficult to use effectively, and as a result a trail was developed that avoided the rugged canyons of the Colorado River that Armijo crossed. The new route pioneered by William Wolfskill and George C. Yount in 1831 had the advantage of better water and pasture resources for the caravans. This route, known today as the Northern (Main) Route, was the most heavily used and offered a third trade item: Indian slaves, who were sold as domestic servants, mainly in Santa Fe.

Using this guide, modern-day adventurers can travel along the roads and highways of Utah and Arizona which parallel or overlie the historic routes, and can experience many sites and points of interest associated with the Old Spanish National Historic Trail.

*Mexican arrieros depicted in a 1836 lithograph - Frédéric Lehnert/Carl Nebel*

# Old Spanish Trail - Armijo Route 1829 & 1830

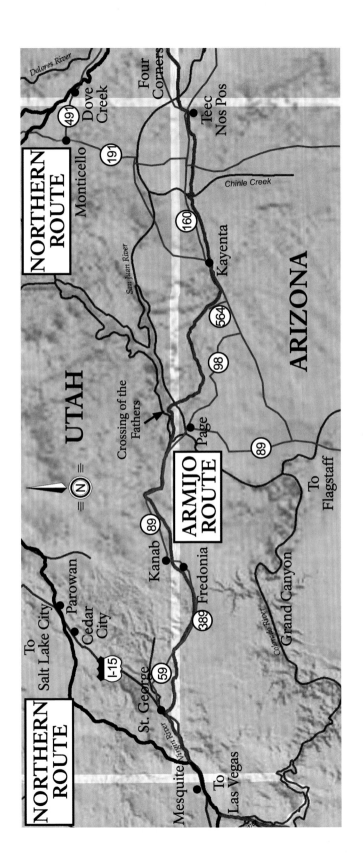

# Four Corners to Mesquite, Nevada: The Armijo Route

The tour of the Armijo Route begins at the Four Corners Monument which can be reached via US 64 from Shiprock, New Mexico, or US 160 from Cortez, Colorado.

*A-1: Four Corners Monument, where the states of Utah, Arizona, New Mexico, and Colorado meet*

The famous Four Corners Monument was created by surveyors in 1875. Armijo and his caravan left the San Juan River on November 22, 1829, and passed near this spot on their way to California. The Navajo Nation controls the area surrounding the monument and charges an admission fee. It is unique since it is the only place in the United States where you can be in four states at the same time. From the monument, travel south to US 160 and head west toward Teec Nos Pos, Arizona.

*A-2: Teec Nos Pos Trading Post*

This trading post on the Navajo Indian Reservation is home to an important spring that lies on the north side of the Carrizo Mountains. Armijo's party stopped at the spring on November 22, 1829. They traded with the Navajo at a site on the west side of the mountain and secured the services of a Navajo guide.

*Teec Nos Pos Trading Post*

Continue west on US 160. West of the US 191 intersection, the highway crosses Walker Creek between MP 435-436 and Chinle Wash at MP 429, streams that provided water for the Armijo party. Near MP 421 the highway enters the eastern drainage of Laguna Creek. The Armijo route lies along the north side of the highway from this point to Kayenta, Arizona. In 1829, there would have been water in the creek. Modern use of its water has dried the stream.

*Church Rock*

*A-3:  Church Rock  at MP 401–402*

The Armijo caravan traversed this general area on November 27, perhaps setting a campsite in view of this impressive 800-foot-tall volcanic dike. This rock is mostly kimberlite, the green color coming from the mineral olivine. Kimberlite is the source of diamonds in South Africa and Russia. In the Four Corners, the kimberlite contains only tiny pieces of garnet and an occasional peridot. After a photo stop at Church Rock, continue west on Highway 160 to Kayenta, Arizona.

*A-4:  Navajo Code-Talkers Exhibit*

Stop at Burger King in Kayenta to view the Navajo Code Talkers exhibit. You may also want to visit Monument Valley Navajo Tribal Park, one of the most beautiful landscapes in the world. It is about 25 miles north of Kayenta on US 163. The Armijo route continues on Highway 160 west to Marsh Pass at MP 383 then heads north into the rugged canyon country surrounding Navajo Mountain. At MP 374, turn north on Highway 564 to Navajo National Monument.

*A-5:  Navajo National Monument*

The road to Navajo National Monument parallels the Armijo route. Modern-day travelers get a good feel for the type of country the 1829 expedition went through. Check out the historical exhibits at the Visitor Center and be sure to walk to the overview of Betatakin ruin.

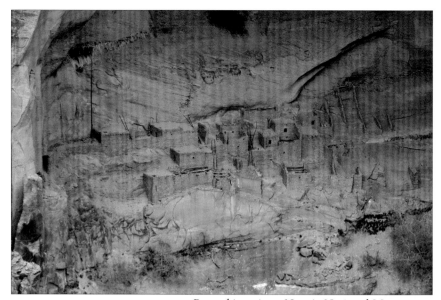
*Betatakin ruin at Navajo National Monument*

Armijo probably did not see the ruin that was abandoned by 1300 AD, as there was no mention of it in his journal. The Passport To Your National Parks stamp is available here. Return to US 160 to continue your road tour.

*A-6: Navajo Mountain Scenic View*

Head west on US 160 toward Tuba City. Between MP 373-374 the highway passes by the Black Mesa coal mines. Coal from the Mesa is used to power the Navajo Generating Station at Page, Arizona. Between MP 361-362 turn north onto AZ 98 toward Page. Navajo Mountain, the 10,000-foot laccolitic mountain to the north, is a major landmark in this area.

The Armijo group followed an Indian trail that is located about half the distance between the highway and the mountain. To get some sense of the ruggedness of the region, stop at the scenic view between MP 343-344 on AZ 98 and look to the north toward Navajo Mountain.

The 10,388-foot-tall peak that dominates the landscape was named by geologist and explorer John Wesley Powell. The local Paiutes refer to it as Paiute Mountain, and Navajos call it Naat sis'áán translated as "Earth Head." Diné Bikéyah (Navajoland) is bounded by sacred mountains to the east, south, west, and north. Within these borders are other mountains and landforms related to Navajo legends. Navajo Mountain is said to represent the head of Earth Woman (Nahasdzáán) and some traditional Navajos refuse to climb the mountain above the lower elevations.

*A-7: John Wesley Powell Museum – Page, Arizona*

The distance to the Old Spanish Trail narrows substantially as you approach Leche-e Rock at MP 308. The Navajo Generating Station with Tower Butte in the background is on the right at MP 301. The Armijo route passes between Tower Butte and Boundary Butte (the cliffs in the background). At the traffic light, turn right onto Coppermine Road and right again onto Lake Powell Boulevard. The Powell Museum is on your right at the intersection with North Navajo Drive. A visit to the museum is a must stop for Old Spanish Trail visitors.

*Grandview Knoll vista*

After your visit to the museum, go to the Grandview Knoll near the Lake View Elementary School. At the museum, travel northeast on North Navajo Drive approximately 1 mile to 20th Avenue. Turn right and proceed east along the north side of Lake View Elementary School to the corner of 20th Avenue and Grandview Street. Turn left and drive atop Grandview Knoll (36°55'59.7"N  111°27'30.6"W).

From the top of the nearby knoll are excellent views of Lake Powell and Tower, Gunsight, and Boundary Buttes. The Armijo party traveled along the line of cliffs visible to the east and north leading to and from the Crossing of the Fathers (Ute Ford). This place on the Colorado River was named after the Dominguez-Escalante expedition who used the ford in 1776 on their return to Santa Fe. Gunsight Butte on Lake Powell, visible to the northeast, lies directly on the path to the historic river crossing which now lies under Lake Powell.

*A-8: Glen Canyon Dam Visitor Center*

From downtown Page, follow Lake Powell Boulevard off the hill to US 89. Turn right onto the highway and head toward Kanab,

*Glen Canyon Dam*

Utah. Cross the 800-foot-high steel bridge across the Colorado River to the Glen Canyon Dam Visitor Center. Inside the center, be sure to examine the map diorama and locate the site of the Crossing of the Fathers, in Padre Bay. The Armijo caravan crossed the Colorado River at this point in 1829. Visit the book store operated by the Glen Canyon Natural History Association to get your Old Spanish Trail passport stamp and browse a wide selection of hiking- and history-themed books. After your Visitor Center experience, walk outside to see the Colorado River Gorge and Glen Canyon Dam. You will immediately understand the difficulty earlier travelers had in getting across the Colorado River and its canyons. Before you leave the center, you may also want to take a tour of the dam and its generating station.

*Optional Tour A - Boat Tour to Rainbow Bridge National Monument*

A tour to Rainbow Bridge National Monument is recommended. You will have a close-up view of the many canyons whose waters drain into the

*Rainbow Bridge National Monument*

Colorado River. While boating across Padre Bay the tour guide will note the location of the Crossing of the Fathers and nearby Padre Rock. This is the same historic crossing used by the Armijo party to cross the Colorado River. At Rainbow Bridge you have a close-up view of the 310-foot natural bridge. Information about the boat tour is available at the Glen Canyon Dam Visitor Center, online at www.lakepowell.com, or by calling 928-645-2433. Tours depart from the Lake Powell Resort at Wahweap Marina.

*Optional Tour B – Hike to Horseshoe Bend Overlook*

A one-mile hike to the Horseshoe Bend Overlook south of Page is recommended as a two-hour excursion. From the city of Page, drive south on Highway 89 to between MP 544-545. Look for the exit lane and prominent dirt road on the west side of the road, which leads to a parking area (36 52' 34.37"N 111 30'10.32"W). Walk the rock and sand trail to an outstanding, much-photographed, panoramic view of Glen Canyon below the dam. When you reach the precipice edge you will be looking down 1,000 feet of Navajo Sandstone to a sweeping horseshoe bend of the Colorado River. Even though this is a short hike, be sure to take plenty of water as the sandy trail has no shade and can be hot in the summer season.

*Horseshoe Bend © Christopher K. Eaton Photography*

The view reminds us that historic navigation across the Colorado Plateau was challenging due to steep canyon walls that stretched for hundreds of miles below Green River, Utah, and down through Cataract Canyon, Glen Canyon, Marble Canyon, and the Grand Canyon. Without a boat to ferry across the Colorado River, there were few suitable river crossings for humans and livestock venturing across this region.

*A-9: Lake Powell Scenic View*

Just before leaving Arizona on US 89 between MP 552-553, drive to the top of the Wahweap Grand View for a magnificent view of the west side of Lake Powell (36°57'57.3"N, 111°30'40.0"W). This view shows clearly the direction that Armijo traveled as he headed west through what he called "Blanco Canyon." Today it is called Wahweap Creek and is accessible off the Lone Rock road east of US 89.

*Wahweap Grand View*

*A-10: Grand Staircase-Escalante National Monument Visitor Center*

You may want to stop and visit the Bureau of Land Management's Big Water Visitor Center at Big Water, Utah, which features an impressive dinosaur exhibit. The Center is located on the west side of US 89 between MP 7-8 (37°04'36.6"N 111°39'47.2"W). The Passport To Your National Parks stamp is available here.

*A-11: Paria/Pahreah Historic View Point*

After crossing Clark Bench just north of the highway, the Old Spanish Trail drops into the Paria River drainage. US 89 lies over the trail in this area and reaches the river at MP 21. Just west of the river, Armijo's caravan encountered the hogback cliffs of what today are called "The Cockscomb." The drive through the cliffs demonstrates

*The Cockscomb*

clearly the problem Armijo faced and why his mule train probably followed the river to avoid the obstacle, although there is debate whether the party might have used a short cut through the ridge.

Continue on US 89 to roadside signage at Paria/Pahreah between MP 30-31 (37°11'09.6"N 111°59'44.9"W). The signs have information about the Old Spanish Trail and tell the story of the historic Pahreah townsite and the more recent movie sets at Paria.

The Pahreah town-site can only be reached by following the dirt road down to the river from this point. The road is five miles long, and becomes rather steep and twisting near the end. Road conditions vary, and high clearance

*Road to Pahreah*

vehicles may be advisable on the road. It should not be traveled in wet weather. It is definitely worth the drive down to the river for beautiful views of Chinle formation striated rocks. When standing at the Paria River, you can envision Armijo's route as it might have emerged from a box canyon cutting through the Cockscomb formation.

Numerous floods have washed away most of the historic townsite which was located across the river. The Pahreah cemetery with burials from 1877-1892 is located on the west side of the river near the road's end. It is a reminder of the small group of tenacious pioneers who settled at the Pahreah townsite and attempted to battle the elements and control the Paria River. Twenty graves are marked.

*A-12: Grand Staircase-Escalante National Monument - Kanab, Utah*
    The Armijo party followed the Vermillion Cliffs, the same cliffs that determine the present route of the highway into Kanab. There are several Anasazi Indian villages and numerous campsites along this section of the trail. A small village, which may be the "Red Pueblo" referred to in the sketchy Armijo journal, is located near Flag Point. From this spot near MP 52, the Armijo party may have gone directly west to Kanab Creek in Kanab. More likely, they followed the path of least resistance down open valleys to the southwest and crossed Kanab Creek a short distance south of Fredonia, Arizona. A second Grand Staircase-Escalante National Monument Visitor Center is located on the north side of the highway as you enter Kanab. It features archaeology and geology exhibits about the Monument. The Passport To Your National Parks stamp is available here.

*A-13: Red Pueblo Museum - Fredonia, Arizona*
    At the junction of US highway 89 and 89A in Kanab, turn south to Fredonia, Arizona, on US 89A. Between MP 611-610, on the north end of Fredonia, watch for the Red Pueblo Museum on your left (36°57'44.3"N 112°31'37.2"W). It has an excellent collection of Anasazi Indian artifacts and information on the Old Spanish Trail. The museum was named after the ruin that Armijo's group reported east of Kanab in 1829.

*A-14: Dominguez-Escalante Historic Monument - Fredonia, Arizona*
    Before leaving Fredonia, drive south to the small Fredonia Roadside Park located a quarter-mile south of the junction of AZ 389 and US 89A (36°56'32.7"N 112°31'32.9"W). The monuments here describe the journey of Dominguez and Escalante in this area. Armijo

was using information provided by the 1776 Dominguez-Escalante party to guide his caravan. To continue, return to the AZ 389/US 89A intersection and drive west on AZ 389 toward Hurricane, Utah, and Pipe Spring National Monument. As you leave Fredonia, you will cross Kanab Creek. Armijo's party called it Ram Creek.

*A-15:  Pipe Spring National Monument - Arizona*
   About 14 miles west of Fredonia is the turnoff to Pipe Spring

National Monument adjacent to the headquarters for the Kaibab Band of Paiute Indians (36°51'28.8"N 112°44'08.1"W). The Visitor Center at the monument has a display panel on 19th century contacts and slavery along the Spanish Trail. The springs were utilized by Southern

*Pipe Spring*

Paiutes until the Mormons built structures here for defense during the Mormon-Navajo War and as a major tithing ranch. Armijo called the spring "Agua de la Vieja" (Water of the Old Woman) and camped here on December 15, 1829. The Passport To Your National Parks stamp is available here.

*A-16:  Highway 389 Western View Stop - Arizona*
   AZ 389 overlies the Armijo route to about MP 10. Between MP 9-8 (36°53'38.0"N 112°54'52.0"W), stop on the west side of the road at the BLM viewing site to read the interpretative signs about the Honeymoon Trail and the Arizona Strip, and look at the region Armijo called "Coyote Plains." One can guess what his group saw as they crossed this waterless region headed west. At Colorado City, Arizona, AZ 389 becomes UT 59 as it enters Utah. As you drive into Hurricane, Utah, note the rugged drop of the cliffs. It took Armijo's group two days to find the only pack animal path off the cliffs. It is

located about 13 miles south of Hurricane.

*A-17:   Hurricane City Museum and Park - Hurricane, Utah*
         The next stop on our journey is at the junction of UT 59
and UT 9 (37°10'32.8"N 113°17'17.0"W). The Hurricane City
Museum and Park is located here, and contains a number of historic
monuments, including another Dominguez-Escalante monument
placed here in 1976. A side trip to Zion National Park is only a thirty-
minute drive from the museum. If you choose not to take the optional
Warner Valley drive, skip to waypoint A-18 in this guide.

*Optional Warner Valley Scenic and Historic Drive - approximately 25-35
miles depending on your explorations.*

*Warner Valley*

For travelers with high clearance vehicles, a trip from Hurricane south
to Warner Valley and then west to St. George provides an excellent
opportunity to see the original Armijo route as it may have appeared
in 1829. Ask locally for road conditions. A wind storm might deposit
an impassable foot of sand across the road. At other times, the road
may be drivable in a low-clearance vehicle. Never take the route in wet
weather, and always carry water when traveling this route.

From the Hurricane City Museum, drive west on Main Street to 700 West (look for the sign to the airport) and turn south (37°10'34.6"N 113°18'00.2"W). Follow 700 West south for 6.4 miles past Sky Ranch. The pavement ends here. Continue south on the gravel/dirt road for another 2.2 miles where it splits. One gravel road continues straight south and the other turns right (37°03'30.26"N 113°18'22.80"W). A sign directs you to the right to Warner Valley, Dinosaur Track Site, and Fort Pearce.

You will need to return to this spot, but first follow the road straight south for 4.5 miles and arrive at the base of what is called the "Honeymoon Trail." The sign at the base of the road explains the unusual name. A four-wheel drive or walk up the road gives you a great view of Warner Valley to the west and the road just driven from Hurricane. On a clear day you can see the water pools from springs to the west at what is now called Fort Pearce. Armijo called the spring "Stinking Water Spring. "

After examining the path off the 1,000-foot Hurricane Cliffs, drive

*Top: Intersection of dinosaur tracks or Fort Pearce. Bottom: Dinosaur tracks*

back to where the road split and drive southwest then west (left) through Warner Valley. You may want to take the 1.1 mile diversion to the Warner Valley Dinosaur Tracks. Watch for the signs directing you to them; at the T intersection, take the east turn (right).

If you opt out of viewing the dinosaur tracks, turn west (left) toward Fort Pearce. Approximately 17 miles into your drive you will come to signs directing you to Fort Pearce just south of the main road. You will first see a hiking route to the fort, but continue for .4 miles to a parking lot and easy access to the fort.

The fort was constructed by Mormons in 1861, just 32 years after Armijo passed here. The pools from the spring can be seen from the south side of the partially reconstructed fort. This is the largest riparian zone in this wash. Armijo's group traveled on west toward the Virgin River by following Fort Pearce Wash.

*Fort Pearce Wash*

Return to the main dirt road and head west toward St. George. Drifting sand dunes in this area between the Fort Pearce turnoff and the St. George airport road to the west may cause the roads to meander. If the roads become confusing, drive toward the large "D" on the hills to the west if you can see it. (The southwestern corner of the state is known as "Utah's Dixie.") The dirt/gravel road ends at UT 7 with easy access to I-15 South. From here, it is approximately 13 miles to St. George and the US Forest Service/ BLM Information Center and the Dixie Convention Center, where this guide continues at A-18.

*A-18: St. George Forest Service/BLM Information Center – St. George*
      From the Hurricane City Museum and Park, head west on

State Street, UT 9, toward St. George, Utah. UT 9 ends at Interstate 15 about 12 miles to the west. Head south on I-15 toward St. George and take the Bluff Street exit (Exit 6). Turn left (east) at Bluff Street and continue directly onto Riverside Drive. The information center is located on the left at 345 E. Riverside Drive. The center has information on the history of the Old Spanish Trail and an excellent selection of books about the trail as well as other area attractions (37°04'56.9"N 113°34'35.8"W). The Passport To Your National Parks stamp is available here.

## A-19: Junction of Virgin and Santa Clara Rivers

From the information center turn southwest onto Riverside Drive. At the first traffic light turn left onto Dixie Drive. The junction of Fort Pearce Wash and the Virgin River is on the left side of the road. It is difficult to see unless you walk through the tamarisk to the Virgin River. Take the exit into the Dixie Center St. George Convention Center, 120 East Street (37°04'31.8"N 113°34'52.1"W), before crossing I-15. At the convention center turn right off Dixie Drive and proceed to the parking lot. Drive to the west end of the parking lot and turn left under the Dixie Drive overpass toward Confluence Park.

Walk down the hiking/biking trail to the junction of the Virgin and Santa Clara Rivers. From the junction of the Virgin and Santa Clara Rivers you can imagine Armijo going straight west to the mountain, then south around it. The Northern Route (which you can follow along I-70 and I-15, see pages 26, 34-56) came in to the north end of the mountain and went around it on the west side. The fur trapper and explorer Jedediah Smith came to this spot in 1826 and again in 1827. Smith's party journeyed down the Virgin River in 1826 but the next year traveled up "Corn Creek" (Santa Clara River) and over Utah Hill (Old Highway 91). The route over Utah Hill, about 30 miles to the west, became the main route for Old Spanish Trail travelers.

## A-20: Virgin River Gorge, Arizona I-15 Exit

After your visit to the river junction, return to your vehicle and take I-15 south through the Virgin River Gorge. This part of the interstate highway system was not completed until 1974. The narrow sections cost over one million dollars per mile. At the time, it was the most expensive interstate highway in the country. The interstate crosses the Virgin River nine times before exiting the Gorge. The Virgin River Canyon Recreation Area at Cedar Pocket (Exit 18) as you travel through the canyon offers picnic and camping facilities amid tall rock formations. After you have driven through the canyon and are on the plains, leave the freeway (Exit 8) as you cross the river for the last time. Turn south (left) under the freeway onto Old Highway 91 and travel south to look at the Virgin River to the east (left). The Armijo Route and the Northern Route followed the river for the next 20 miles.

*Virgin River Gorge*

*A-21: Nevada Information Center - Mesquite, Nevada*

Continue south on Old Highway 91 along the river. It becomes very clear why Old Spanish Trail travelers stayed on the river. The canyons to the west are too deep and rugged for travel. The Armijo route leaves Arizona at the informative Old Spanish Trail sign in front of the Nevada Information Center in Mesquite. The center is located a short distance from the Arizona/Nevada state line.

You have reached the westernmost part of the Armijo Route through Utah and Arizona. Armijo continued on to what is now Los Angeles on a route running south of Las Vegas to Tecopa, Barstow, and San Bernardino, California, before reaching Los Angeles.

**To continue exploring the Old Spanish Trail in Utah**, follow this guide's Northern Route, driving from St. George, Utah, up through Green River. At Green River you have a choice of continuing the Northern Route through Moab, Utah and Durango, Colorado to Santa Fe, New Mexico, or taking the North Branch through Grand Junction, Gunnison, and San Luis, Colorado, before arriving in Santa Fe.

# Old Spanish Trail - Northern Route 1830-1848
## Dove Creek, Colorado to Green River, Utah

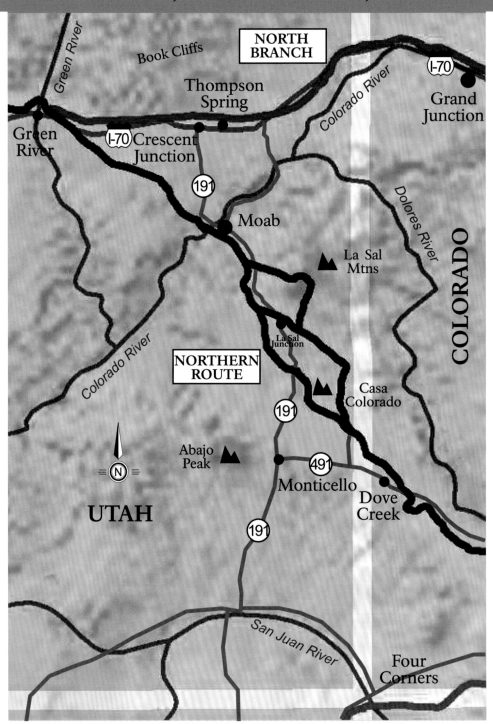

## Monticello, Utah, through Moab to I-70: The Northern Route

This route is part of the Northern Route of the Old Spanish Trail and connects with the North Branch coming from Grand Junction, Colorado, along present-day I-70. The Northern Route began in Santa Fe and continued northwest through present-day Durango, Colorado, and onward to the Colorado/Utah border, where we join it.

*N-1: Colorado-Utah Viewpoint*
Our journey along the Northern Route of the trail through Utah begins at the Colorado/Utah border on US 491, east of Monticello, Utah. Stop at the boundary sign on the highway and observe the La Sal Mountains to the northwest. The trail crosses from Colorado into Utah a few miles north of this place. Nineteenth-century travelers used the mountains as a guide for the direction they should travel. By staying on a course toward the western side of the mountains, they avoided the impassable

*La Sal Mountains*

canyon country farther west.

Drive west on Highway 491 to Monticello, then turn north on US 191 toward Moab. The BLM office in Monticello on US 191, left side of the road (look for the flag), has a relief topo map of the area. You can also purchase the BLM surface management map of the La Sal area. The Passport To Your National Parks stamp is available here.

*N-2: Church Rock Viewpoint*
Drive 14 miles north of Monticello to a highway pull-off that offers a view of the massive Church Rock. The Old Spanish Trail passed on the east against the cliffs in a northwestern direction.

*Church Rock near Monticello*

Spanish Trail travelers regularly camped behind the sandstone dome to the east of Church Rock. If you have extra time, drive west on US 211 to Newspaper Rock State Historical Monument for one of the most remarkable Indian petroglyphs sites in the state. It is 12 miles from US 191 (37°59'18.1"N 109°31'05.3"W). If you have more time, travel 22 miles farther on US 211 to visit the Needles section of Canyon-lands National Park.

*Newspaper Rock*

*Casa Colorado*

### N-3: Casa Colorado Sandstone Dome

From the Church Rock viewpoint, drive north on US 191 to Steen Road, located between MP 95-96. Look for the sign "OHV Trailhead" and turn—that is Steen Road, indicated by a small San Juan County

114 sign (38°12'06.9"N 109°22.27.3"W). Drive east about 3.6 miles on Steen Road for a close-up of Casa Colorado. Its southwest-facing alcoves and natural water tanks made it one of the most important camping sites along the trail. The road is on the north and west side of Casa Colorado, so you won't see the alcoves unless you hike around to the southwest side.

*N-4: Wilson Arch and Kane Springs Rest Stop*
From Casa Colorado, the Spanish Trail closely follows the road back to highway 191 and then heads north along the west side of the highway. Stop at Wilson Arch (38°16'24.7"N 109°22'20.9"W), which is adjacent to the highway. A parking area allows travelers to photograph and hike to this impressive natural arch. Most Spanish Trail travelers likely missed the arch since the trail was beyond the rocky hills to the west of the arch. But they may have stopped at the Looking Glass Arch to the west. Unfortunately this arch is not visible from US 191, but is mentioned on a sign at the rest stop.

*Wilson Arch*

After your stop at Wilson Arch, continue north on US 191. You may want to stop at the commercial property called Hole N' the Rock. It has a historic sign in the parking lot which mentions the Spanish Trail. Just beyond Hole N' the Rock, you come to the Kane Springs highway rest stop where, years earlier, Spanish Trail travelers drank from a spring. There is also an Old Spanish Trail sign at the rest stop. Continue on US 191 to Moab.

*N-5: Moab Historic Sites*

As you enter Moab from the south, the influence of the Old Spanish Trail becomes evident. The valley that the road follows to the Colorado River is called Spanish Valley and you will notice names like Spanish Trail Arena and Old Spanish Trail Trailer Park.

At the south edge of town, you may want to visit the Old City Park which has a small plaque about the Spanish Trail. The plaque has a sketch of historic Casa Colorado and Looking Glass Rock. To find the park, turn off US 191 at Spanish Trail Road (across from Spanish Trail RV Park and across from the impressive cliffs to the west) (38°52'8"N 109°50'4"W), drive east across the river to Murphy Lane, turn left on Highland Drive to the park (38°53'97.0"N 109°49'70.2"W).

The BLM office is in downtown Moab at 82 Dogwood Ave. Be sure to stop at the Visitor Information Center at Main and Center Streets (look for the blue sign on US 191), where you can get your Passport To Your National Parks stamp. The Center has extensive information and literature about the area and the trail, including books and souvenirs for purchase. Two blocks east of the information center you will find the Dan O' Laurie Museum at 118 E. Center Street, with historic displays about the area. Their *Canyon Legacy* publication featured the history of the trail in Volume 53, Spring 2005.

*Colorado River*

The next major stop is at Lions Park located on the Colorado River at the intersection of US 191 and US 128 E (38°60'23.9"N 109°57'56.5"W). Use the parking lot close to the river, not the bike trail hub. You'll see several Old Spanish Trail interpretative signs. Walk across the bike trail bridge and you will appreciate the difficulty Spanish Trail travelers had in getting across the river.

If you would like to hike the Spanish Trail, continue toward Arches National Park on US 191. Look for the "MOAB, AGAIN & AGAIN" sign on the mountain side of the road (right side as you leave town), and turn into the parking lot by the sign. Signage indicates where to hike down the river below the bike trail bridge and on into Arches National Park along Courthouse Wash. Beware of quicksand along the river.

*N-6:  Arches National Park*

The next stop is at Arches National Park located three miles north of Moab and the Colorado River. The Old Spanish Trail traveled from the Colorado River up Courthouse Wash through the southern end of the park. View the Trail exhibit at the Visitor Center. The Passport To Your National Parks stamp is available here. Drive 4.7 miles into the park to see Courthouse Wash, where the Old Spanish Trail traversed along the bottom of the wash. After viewing the incredible places in the National Park, head back to US 191. Some Spanish Trail travelers likely enjoyed the arches and cliffs as much as modern visitors to the park. A few 19th century travelers also traveled up the wash (in front of the Visitor Center) and followed the route of the highway northward and avoided the main part of what is now the National Park.

After your visit to the park, continue north on US 191, where the historic trail joins the modern road near the Dead Horse Point road (US 313) just south of the Moab Airport. The trail continued northwest across the Green River desert through the Blue Hills. In this region, Mexican traders used the La Sal Mountains and the Book Cliffs near Green River to guide them to the Green River crossing. Our highway route follows Highway 191 north to its junction with I-70 then west on the freeway to the town of Green River.

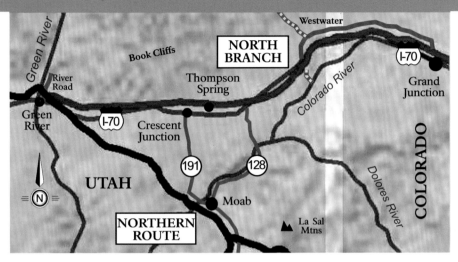

## I-70 from Colorado Border to Green River, Utah: North Branch Segment

The North Branch of the Old Spanish Trail began in Santa Fe and traveled north into Colorado through present-day San Luis and Gunnison, then made its way to Grand Junction. It was mostly a trappers trail to northeastern Utah, but some used it as an alternate route to California. Present-day I-70 follows the Old Spanish Trail from Grand Junction along the Colorado River, then, when the canyons became impossible to cross, the trail entered the badlands along today's freeway south of the Book Cliffs. The trail and Interstate 70 continue from the Utah-Colorado state line to Green River, Utah, where the North Branch joins the Northern Route of the Old Spanish Trail.

*NB-1: Westwater Canyon*

At Exit 227, six miles west of the Colorado border, you can access Westwater Canyon, a major connection to various trapper routes into northern Utah. A nine-mile drive off the freeway takes you to the Colorado River, where there are a ranger station, picnic tables under cottonwood trees, restrooms, and a boat ramp (39°08'64.7"N 109°10'13.6"W). Westwater Canyon today is known for its whitewater boating. National Geographic called the canyon "the best short whitewater trip in the west," according to a sign at the river. The Westwater Creek was a major source of water for travelers on this desolate section of the historic trail. You'll cross it near MP 223 after you return to I-70.

*NB-2: Utah Welcome Center I-70 East*

For west-bound travelers on I-70, the Utah Welcome Center, past exit 190, one mile east of Thompson Springs, has an observation hill, which provides an excellent overview of the country that Spanish Trail travelers had to pass through on their way across this region. An Old Spanish Trail Association brochure can be obtained at the center. This center cannot be accessed by eastbound I-70 travelers. Eastbound travelers may want to stop at a safe pullout in this region for a similar view of the La Sal Mountains to the south.

*NB-3: Thompson Springs and Sego Canyon Glyphs*

Take exit 187 to Thompson Springs (38°57'49.7"N 109°43'21.2"W). The springs were essential for Spanish Trail travelers. The springs have been a major water source for centuries, and also provided water for limited feed for caravan animals in this area. Drive UT 94 north through town and continue over the railroad tracks for 4 miles into Sego Canyon to see the Indian glyphs near the springs (39°01'05.5"N 109°42'37.2"W). The impressive glyphs date from 7000 BC. Don't pass up this drive, which is definitely worth the time. The paved road ends at an arroyo just before the pictographs, with a parking area on the other side of the arroyo. Do not cross the arroyo if it has running water in it.

*Westwater Canyon*

The Northern Route and the North Branch of the Old Spanish Trail join some-where near MP 170. Continue on I-70 to Green River, Utah.

# Old Spanish Trail - Northern Route 1830-1848
## Green River to Fremont Junction (I-70 Exit 86)

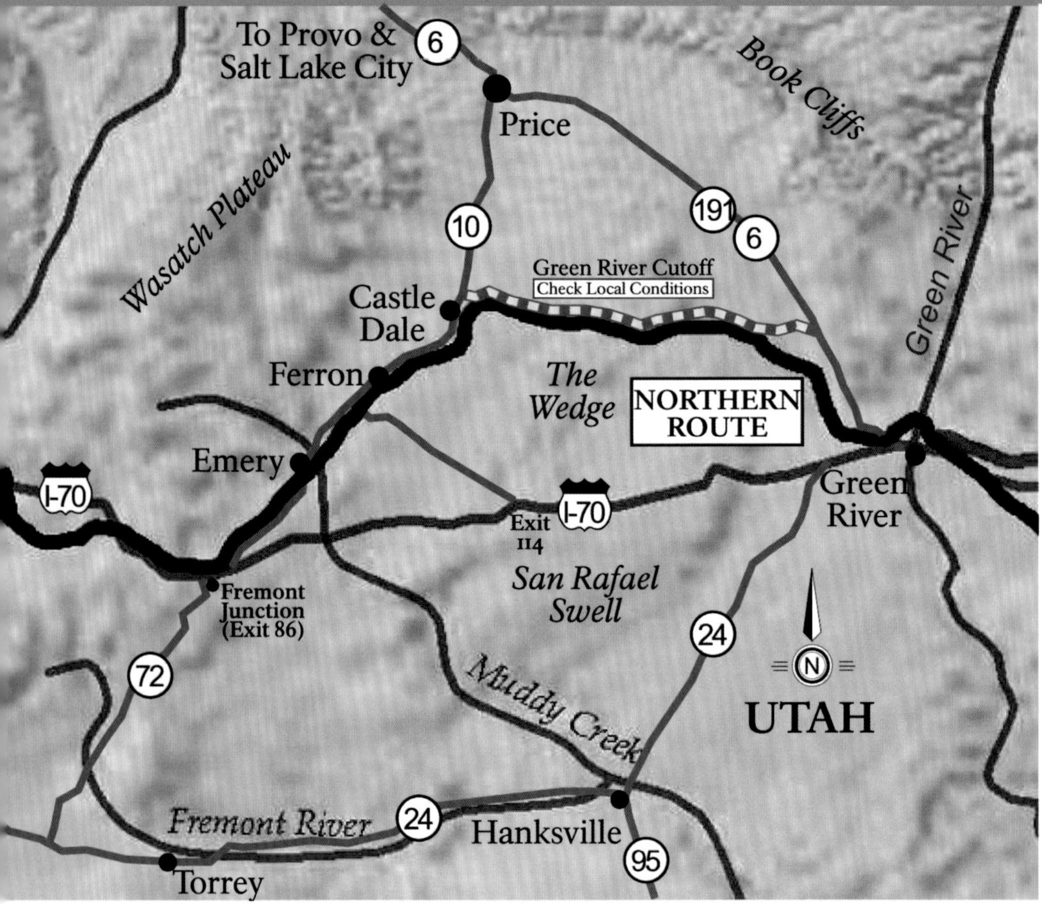

To Provo & Salt Lake City (6)

Book Cliffs

Price

Wasatch Plateau

(10)

(191) (6)

Green River Cutoff
Check Local Conditions

Green River

Castle Dale

Ferron

The Wedge

NORTHERN ROUTE

Emery

I-70

Exit 114  I-70

San Rafael Swell

Green River

Fremont Junction (Exit 86)

(72)

(24)

N

UTAH

Muddy Creek

Fremont River  (24)  Hanksville  (95)

Torrey

## Green River to I-70, Exit 86, Fremont Junction: The Northern Route

The Northern Route of the Old Spanish Trail began in Santa Fe and continued northwest through present-day Durango, Colorado, and onward to the Colorado/Utah border. In Utah, it followed present-day US 191 through Moab to I-70 (page 26), and then led westward along present-day I-70, south down through St. George and into Nevada. The North Branch of the Old Spanish Trail entered eastern Utah along current I-70 (page 32) and met the Northern Route in Green River, Utah.

*Green River silhouettes*

*N-7: Green River and John Wesley Powell River Museum*
　　　Take the I-70 exit 164 into the town of Green River. At the Green River welcome sign, look up the hill and notice the metal trail rider silhouettes. They were placed there by the San Rafael Chapter of the Old Spanish Trail Association. The John Wesley Powell River History Museum is on the north side of the road next to the river. Stop at the museum even if it is not open. The exterior canopy covers more than 20 historic signs describing the area and one is devoted to the Old Spanish Trail. Another sign features the San Rafael Swell, which westbound travelers will be crossing soon. The museum has numerous books and guides about the trail and other unique places in the area, including a topographic map. The Passport To Your National Parks stamp is available here.

After your visit in the museum, you may want to drive to the area near a Green River crossing of the trail. From the museum turn left (east) and drive .3 mile to Hastings Road (38°59'30.8"N 110°08'01.7"W). Turn left onto the road and drive 2.3 miles north. A small wooden sign marks the site of this important spot on the Spanish Trail. It is located past the bend in the river near the road. Look for a dirt road leading in the direction of the river, with a gate flanked by tall trees with a no trespassing sign. The Old Spanish Trail sign is beside the trees (39°01'34.3"N 110°08'21.3"W). Crossing

*OST Green River crossing sign*

the river could delay a party for weeks if the water was high.

Note the excellent view (on a clear day) of the La Sal Mountains to the southeast as you return to Green River. Spanish Trail travelers knew immediately which way to go after they crossed the river. The difficult San Rafael Swell loomed large in the west.

After visiting the sites in Green River, you have two options. Both routes will lead to I-70, Exit 86, where another set of options is available.

Option 1, I-70: This route goes through one of the more scenic stretches, including the San Rafael Swell, of the interstate system. There are no services along I-70 for the next 100 miles, so refresh your necessities at Green River.

Option 2, Green River Cutoff (GRCO): This 44-mile dirt road, about 16 miles north of the interstate, makes an arch around the north end of the San Rafael Swell west to Castle Dale. A high clearance vehicle is recommended, and the route can't be driven in wet weather. The route is a close approximation of the actual trail. Scenic side trips include The Wedge and Little Grand Canyon.

## Option 1: I-70 through San Rafael Swell

The San Rafael Swell is a Navajo Sandstone anticline, a huge dome formed by pressure from underneath the earth's surface over 70 million years ago. Its striking ridge-like rock formations were a major barrier to early 18th and 19th century traffic. Until I-70 was completed, it was impossible to get through. The scenic San Rafael Swell area has been considered as a possible national monument.

*San Rafael Swell: Spotted Wolf viewpoint*

*N-8: San Rafael Swell/View Areas on I-70*

Drive through the city of Green River and return to the interstate on the west side of town. Continue west on I-70 to the Black Dragon Canyon View Area at MP 146. It becomes very clear what the challenge was for Old Spanish Trail trading caravans headed northwest after they crossed the Green River. Another vista for westbound travelers is the viewpoint between MP 142-143. Eastbound travelers will catch their first glimpse of the San Rafael Swell at MP 139 and should stop at the spectacular Spotted Wolf Viewpoint just before MP 143 (38°55'57.9"N 110°28'18.6"W).

*N-9: Museum of the San Rafael - Castle Dale*

Continue west on I-70 to the Moore exit 116. At the exit you may want to stop at another view area, a short distance to the right. Return to the road to Moore and travel northwest about 19 miles toward Castle Dale. Looking to the north gives you a great view of the terrain of Old Spanish Trail on the west side of the San Rafael Swell. Near US 10, you cross the Molen Reef, where a number of petroglyphs and dinosaur tracks have been found. At US 10, drive north past the Hunter Power plant near Ferron to Castle Dale.

Locate the Museum of the San Rafael in Castle Dale, a half block north of Main Street. In addition to pioneer, natural history, and dinosaur exhibits, the museum has an Old Spanish Trail exhibit that includes artifacts dating to the time of the trail's use.

*Muesum of the San Rafael*

To drive the Green River Cutoff road from Castle Dale, travel one mile north of town and look for the brown sign "San Rafael Recreational Access" and a large wooden corral to your right. Turn right on that dirt road, which is the GRCO. The road to the Buckhorn Information Center and The Wedge and Little Grand Canyon, (see description in the Option 2 GRCO

*GRCO sign north of Castle Dale*

route) about an 18-minute drive, is a dirt road but well-maintained and can be driven by any vehicle if the road is not wet. To continue to Buckhorn Wash Road, see GRCO - 3 description.

*N-10: Return to I-70*

From Castle Dale, return south on US 10 toward I-70. This 40-mile drive closely follows the trade trail to the head of Salina Canyon. Jedediah Smith followed this route in 1826. Turn west onto I-70, then take exit 86.

## Option 2: Green River Cutoff (GRCO)

Driving time on dirt road: 2 hours, including photo stops, to The Wedge, 18 minutes from the intersection of The Wedge/GRCO to Castle Dale.

This route includes a well-maintained 44-mile dirt road and requires a high-clearance vehicle, but is a close approximation of the actual trail.

*East end of Green River Cutoff*

Do not take this road in wet weather, as it has a number of arroyos to cross in the eastern section of the road. The western two-thirds of the route is dirt, but not as rough, and can be driven in any vehicle if the road isn't wet, although conditions will vary. Road signs at both ends of the route warn that the road may be impassable in inclement weather.

Travel west three miles from Green River on I-70. Take exit 157, US 6 heading north toward Price. Continue 17 miles to the junction of the Green River Cutoff Road. There is no road sign marking the turnoff, which is a left turn toward the hills (39°11'43.41"N 110°20'18.52"W). You'll know you are on the correct road if you drive under the railroad crossing about 1.4 miles down the road and then turn sharply NNW. As you reach the Swell, the terrain becomes rocky and the road can be smooth except for arroyo crossings, or may be bumpy.

*GRCO-1: Trail Signs*
Look for an Old
Spanish Trail sign at 13.7 miles
(39°10'46.4"N 110°31'13.4"W),
and a second sign at
(39°09'25.8"N 110°38'30.0"W),
placed by the San Rafael
Chapter of the Old Spanish Trail
Association.

*GRCO–2: Buckhorn Information Center, The Wedge*
At 30.4 miles on the GRCO, you will see the Buckhorn
Information Center, with signage and restrooms, and the road to
The Wedge, which is billed as Little Grand Canyon (39°10'05.5"N
110°45'19.59"W). Stop to read the signs, then drive 6.5 miles to The
Wedge view area, which has picnic tables and camping sites. The view
lives up to its name, and is a beautiful spot for a picnic lunch. Return to
the GRCO, and continue 12.4 miles to Castle Dale.

Photo: Ed Geary

*Buckhorn Information Center*

*GRCO–3: Optional Buckhorn Wash Road*
If you prefer not to continue to Castle Dale, or have driven the
route from Castle Dale east, the Buckhorn Draw Road about a mile
east of the Buckhorn information area is an excellent side trip and

takes you to I-70. The directional sign on the GRCO reads Buckhorn Draw, but the route is labeled Buckhorn Wash on some maps. It is well-maintained, better than the GRCO, and passes through a spectacular gorge with several fine prehistoric rock art panels. This route continues through the heart of the San Rafael Swell to intersect I-70 and then continues on to Temple Mountain and Goblin Valley.

*GRCO–4: Museum of the San Rafael - Castle Dale*
Locate the Museum of the San Rafael in Castle Dale, a half block north of Main Street. In addition to pioneer, natural history, and dinosaur exhibits, the museum has an Old Spanish Trail exhibit that includes artifacts dating to the time of the Trail's use.

From Castle Dale, return south on US 10 toward I-70. This 40-mile drive closely follows the trade trail to the head of Salina Canyon. Jedediah Smith followed this route in 1826. Turn west onto I-70 and drive to exit 86.

The two routes meet at I-70, exit 86, Fremont Junction.

*The Wedge, Little Grand Canyon*

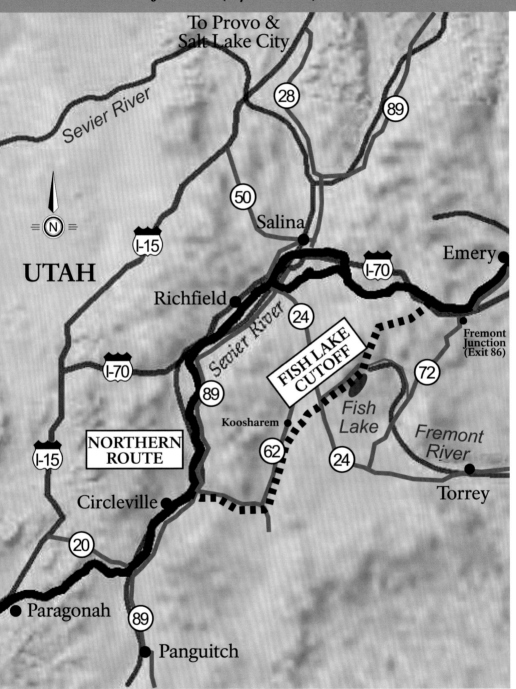

# I-70, Exit 86, Fremont Junction to Circleville

*N-10: Exit 86, Red Creek Old Spanish Trail Kiosk*

Cross to the south side of the freeway and follow the frontage road 1.6 miles west (right) to Red Creek. Here the Fishlake National Forest has an excellent interpretive sign. The Northern Route of the trail left Salina Canyon at this point and, after a very short southward diversion, headed west back into Salina Canyon and on to the Sevier River at Salina. Some Spanish Trail traders and travelers continued southward toward Fish Lake and rejoined the main trail near Circleville.

After viewing the kiosk at Exit 86, you have two options, I-70 or the Fish Lake Cutoff (FLCO). Both end at Circleville.

Option 1: I-70. Includes Richfield and the Fremont Indian State Park, with petroglyph and pictograph viewing trails, and a monument to Jedediah Smith.

Option 2: Fish Lake Cutoff (FLCO). Drive a scenic highway route that closely follows the Fishlake Cutoff from the head of Salina Canyon to Circleville. This route should only be followed from mid-May through October since the road to Fish Lake and UT 72 may not be open due to snow.

## Option 1: I-70 through Richfield

*N-11: Richfield*

       After viewing the Red Creek exhibit, return to I-70 then head west on the interstate. The main trail re-entered Salina Canyon near MP 79, then followed Salt Creek to its junction with the Sevier River at Salina. Continue on I-70 to Richfield.

At Exit 40 turn south onto Main Street in Richfield. At 900 North Street, turn east to the Fishlake National Forest offices located at 115 East 900 North. Information on the area can be obtained here. You can get your Passport To Your National Parks stamp at the BLM Field Office at 150 East 900 North.

*N-12: Traders and Explorers Historic Panel*

       After your visit in Richfield, travel south on Main Street through Richfield and continue south on UT 118. Turn left off the highway to the village of Central Valley. It is a half mile from the highway into the center of town and the Traders and Explorers historic sign across from the large church. In addition to referring to the Old Spanish Trail and early Mormon journeys, the panel honors fur trapper Jedediah Smith, whose early explorations pioneered the western half of the Old Spanish Trail from this area to Los Angeles.

*Jedediah Smith monument*

*N-13: Central Valley - Fremont Indian State Park - Circleville*

From Central Valley, continue south on UT 118 through town then drive southwest toward Elsinore. At Elsinore, return to West I-70 and follow it to exit 17, and the Clear Creek Highway. Drive 3 miles on Clear Creek Highway to the Fremont Indian State Park.

A monument to Jedediah Smith is located on a gravel pull-off. In 1826, Smith and a party of trappers traveled through Red Creek, over Wasatch Pass, and along the Sevier River. He followed Clear Creek to the present-day Fremont Indian State Park. Two miles farther down the Clear Creek Highway is the State Park Visitor Center with artifacts found during the construction of I-70, and a number of trails past petroglyphs and pictographs.

Get back onto I-70 and take exit 23 to US 89. Follow US 89 through Sevier and Marysvale. In 1826, Jedediah Smith went west across the mountains and followed Clear Creek Canyon. I-70 follows or parallels this path to Cove Fort and I-15 (where I-70 ends).

In 1831, however, the Wolfskill party likely followed the river through the narrow Marysvale Canyon where the present-day US 89 is located. It was late in the year of 1831 and passage through the canyon was probably not a major problem since the water would have been low. Most parties, to avoid this canyon with sometimes dangerous high water, traveled straight south of Central Valley, crossed the foothills, and traveled west back to the Sevier River at present-day Marysvale.

*Near Marysville*

After traveling through the canyon, you enter the Big Rock Candy Mountain scenic area. The old trail followed the river from Marysvale on to the town of Junction where the river's major tributary enters. It is now called the East Fork of the Sevier River.

Two miles south of Junction, travelers who chose not to take the Fish Lake Cut-off may want to drive east on UT 62 to the Spanish Trail silhouettes between MP 4-5, a distance of about 4 miles. Return to US 89.

*Silhouettes on UT 62*

Just before you enter Circleville, stop at a pullout to see the mountains in every direction. Mormon explorers in the winter of 1849 and John C. Fremont in the winter of 1853 choose to travel west here rather than follow the Sevier River southward and they nearly froze to death. The main trail led south through Circleville Canyon along the Sevier River.

*Along the Fish Lake Cutoff*

## Option 2: Fish Lake Cutoff (FLCO)

From the Red Creek kiosk at I-70, exit 86, travel east on the frontage road to UT 72 then head southwest toward Loa. UT 72 parallels the Fish Lake Cutoff Trail and both the road and trail cross over 9,000 feet in elevation. The trail followed terrain similar to that through which the road passes. About 25 miles south of I-70, turn right onto the Fremont River Road and drive toward Fish Lake.

*Silhouettes at Fishlake National Forest Interpretive Center*

*FLCO–1: Silhouettes*

About 11 miles from UT 72, arrive at the Fishlake National Forest Old Spanish Trail interpretive signs, a wonderful photo stop with iron caravan silhouettes (38°36'23.6"N 111°37'07.2"W). The Fish Lake Cutoff of the Old Spanish Trail comes from the north at this point. One mile farther west, stop at the Johnson Reservoir historic signs and the scenic view of the lake. Continue west to Fish Lake where the highway becomes UT 25. Caravan travelers in the 1830s and 1840s caught and ate fish from the lake. It was a refreshing change from the normal fare.

*FLCO–2: Fish Lake Lodge*

Stop at the Fish Lake Lodge and visit with Stephanie and Gary Moulton, who have managed the Lodge for over 30 years, and know the Old Spanish Trail and the area very well. Under construction from 1928 until 1933, and built of native spruce logs, the lodge is one of the largest log structures in the United States.

Between MP 7-6 at Doctor Creek Trailhead, stop to see another set of

Old Spanish Trail signs and silhouettes. The highway closely follows the Fish Lake Cutoff through this area and crosses a 9,000+-foot pass on the west. Cutoff travelers descended west off the mountain into the valley below. At the T-junction of UT 25 and 24, turn north on UT 24.

*FLCO–3: Koosharem Reservoir*

Drive about four miles north on UT 24 to Browns Lane—a sign indicates Koosharem. Turn west to Koosharem. At the intersection of Browns Lane and UT 62, turn right (north) and drive about 1.5 miles to Koosharem Reservoir to view a special Old Spanish Trail exhibit placed by the Southern Paiute Koosharem Band, the National Park Service, and the Bureau of Land Management (38°35'59.0"N 111°50'48.8"W).

*Near Koosharem Reservoir*

Return to Koosharem on UT 62 and continue south. The highway follows Otter Creek through Grass Valley. The Fish Lake Cutoff trail followed the creek. UT 62 passes Otter Creek Reservoir and the east branch of the Sevier River. At the junction with UT 22 and UT 62, turn west on UT 62 toward Kingston. The trail follows the river to its junction with the Sevier River.

Between MP 4-5 at Kingston Canyon Recreation Area, stop to read the historic signs and perhaps photograph the third set of iron silhouettes. The Fish Lake Cutoff joins the main trail just west of Kingston where UT 62 crosses the Sevier River and the highway ends at US 89. Turn left (south) onto US 89 toward Circleville.

*Silhouettes on UT 62*

The two routes meet in Circleville.

# Old Spanish Trail - Northern Route 1830-1848
## Circleville to Parowan, Utah

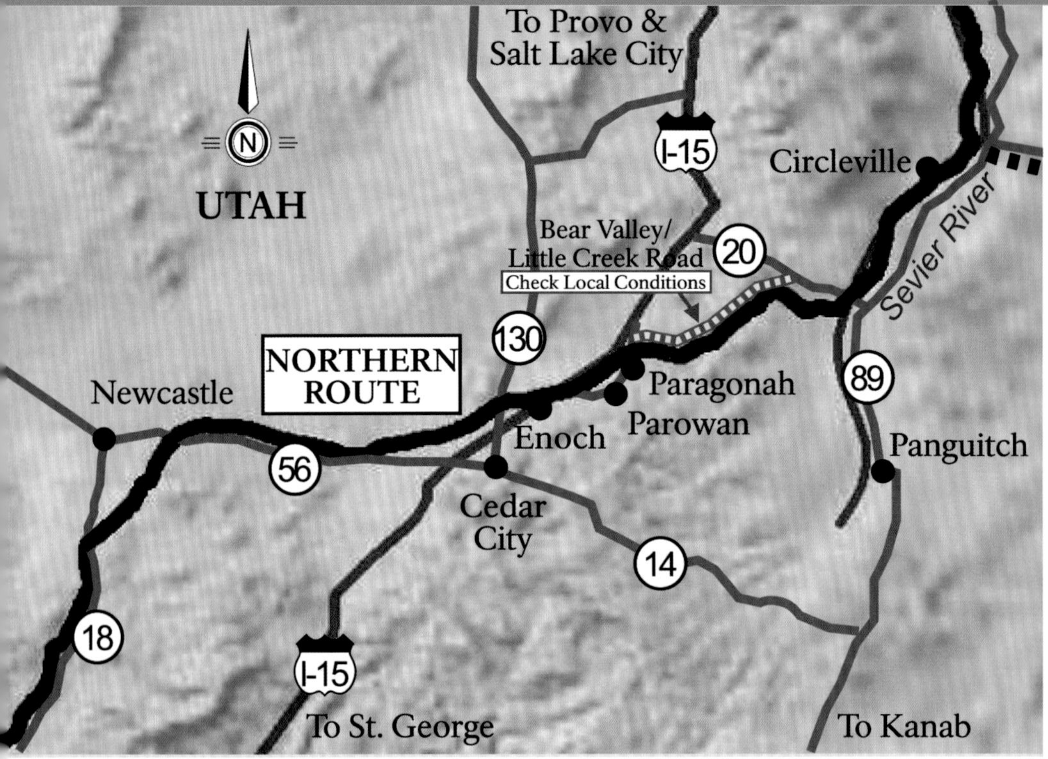

To Provo & Salt Lake City

N

I-15

Circleville

Sevier River

UTAH

Bear Valley/
Little Creek Road
Check Local Conditions

20

130

89

NORTHERN
ROUTE

Paragonah

Newcastle

Parowan

Panguitch

Enoch

56

Cedar
City

14

18

I-15

To St. George

To Kanab

# Circleville to Parowan

*N-14:  Bear Valley Creek Historic Marker*

From Circleville continue south on US 89. Between MP 156-155 are the unmarked remains of Butch Cassidy's boyhood home. Please respect the private property there. The trail and the highway follow the Sevier River from Circleville to the junction of UT 20 and US 89. Turn right onto UT 20 to the west.

In 1831, the Wolfskill party kept going south and were forced to cross the mountains near Panguitch or Hatch. Later parties went along Bear Creek, which UT 20 follows, then south up the creek into the mountains (Option 2: Bear Valley/Little Creek drive). Large herds of horses are partially responsible for the erosion that you should notice on the creek next to the road.

Stop at the junction of Bear Valley Road and UT 20, 6.9 miles from US 89, where you will find an Old Spanish Trail historic marker (38°00'21.4"N 112°30'33.5"W). The road is Bear Valley Road on the map, but the green road sign says Little Creek.

*Junction of Little Creek
Road and UT 20, with
Old Spanish Trail marker*

At this point you have two options.

Option 1: UT 20, I-15 to Parowan. An easy route with a short excursion to the lower end of Little Creek.

Option 2: Bear Valley/ Little Creek to Parowan. This 19-mile dirt road provides one of the best examples of the country that the trail actually passed through. It can be driven in an automobile, but your vehicle will get very dusty. It should not be driven in wet weather and is not open during the winter months.

## Option 1: UT 20, I-15 to Parowan

*N-15: Little Creek/Paragonah*
        Follow UT 20 to its intersection with I-15 and travel south toward Paragonah. There is an expansive view of Bear Creek Valley from UT 20 between MP 10-11. Note the rugged volcanic terrain as you continue west. The Pratt and Fremont expeditions of 1849 and 1854, respectively, had great difficulty crossing this country, which you can see a few miles north of the highway.

At the junction of UT 20 and I-15, you may want to travel five miles north to Exit 100 and read the historic signs on the east side of the freeway. They commemorate the 1849 Mormon Expedition led by Parley P. Pratt from the Spanish Trail at Circleville to the head of the Little Salt Lake. Explorer John C. Fremont followed an identical path in the winter of 1854 and the canyon was named for him.

Travel south on I-15 to the Paragonah exit (Exit 82) and drive south onto Main Street. On the far north end of town, turn east (left) onto Little Creek Road (labeled 700N coming from the north) (37°53'49.2"N 112°46'28.3"W), and drive east on a gravel road toward the cliffs then north (left) toward Little Creek. The two-mile journey takes you to the mouth of Little Creek. The mouth of the canyon is marked by a green water tank.

*Southern end of Little Creek Road*

If you continue driving the dirt road along the stream through the canyon, you will be traveling Option 2: Bear Valley/Little Creek (next page), which ends at UT 20.

Here Ute Indians would trade with Spanish Trail travelers. If the caravan was small, the Indians might eliminate them, or to avoid bloody conflict the Indians might exact a toll. Larger parties would trade woolen goods and horses for Indian slaves. Utes often captured young Paiute Indian children and traded them at the mouth of this narrow canyon. It was a point that traders could not bypass easily. The Indian slaves were sold as domestic servants in both Los Angeles and Santa Fe, but principally in Santa Fe.

Return to Paragonah's Main Street and drive on to Parowan. Old Highway 91 overlies the trail in this area.

## Option 2: Bear Valley/Little Creek to Parowan

From the historic marker on UT 20, head south on Little Creek Road. Nineteenth-century traders stayed closer to Bear Creek on the east side of the valley. The gravel road and the stream meet after about five miles. In addition to snow melt in the creek, Bear Creek is fed by perennial springs. Even in the driest years there is water in the creek.

*Little Creek Road*

About 11.2 miles along the road, travelers pass from Bear Creek into Little Creek over a pass that was on the old trail. The trail is at an elevation of about 8,100 feet. This was the highest elevation of the Northern Route, not including the Fish Lake Cutoff, of the Old Spanish Trail in Utah. Stop to read the sign at the pass (37°54'29.9"N 112°38'12.4"W).

As you descend from the pass, notice the eroded rut on your left that was created by running livestock over the trail. The rut is about five feet beyond the ditch running alongside the road; the rut is in the grass and is about a foot deep and a foot wide. The road turns west as it encounters the upper reaches of Little Creek. The trading trail followed the stream west until it reached the valley of the Little Salt Lake.

Near the 14-mile mark is an inscription that dates back to 1842. It was left by William Knight, who first traveled the trail in 1841, and then emigrated to California from Santa Fe with his family in 1842. The inscription is on the sandstone cliffs on the north side of the creek, a short distance from the water tank at the entrance of Little Creek.

Old Spanish Trail travelers turned southward after exiting the canyon, as does our modern road. Two miles farther, the gravel road reaches Old Highway 91 on the north end of Paragonah. Follow the old highway into Parowan, since it traverses much of the original trail's route.

The two routes meet in Parowan.

*Little Creek Road near summit*

# Old Spanish Trail - Northern Route 1830-1848
## Parowan, Utah to Mesquite, Nevada

UTAH

Bear Valley/
Little Creek Road (20)
Check Local Conditions

NORTHERN
ROUTE (130)

(56)

Paragonah

Enoch Parowan

Newcastle

(56)

I-15 Cedar City

(14)

NEVADA

Mountain Meadow

(18)

(89)

Gunlock

St. George

(9)

Shivwits

(59)

≡ (N) ≡ Kanab (89)

Virgin River

I-15

389 Fredonia

Mesquite

ARMIJO
ROUTE

To Las Vegas

ARIZONA

# Parowan to St. George, Utah, and Mesquite, Nevada

*N-16: Parowan City Park*
 When you reach Parowan, drive south (left) on Main Street (which turns into UT 274, then UT 143) and stop at the Fremont historic marker at 100 South Main, just past the Mormon church. Fremont spent several weeks at the Smith home west of the marker. The Mormon people rescued Fremont's men from certain disaster in a winter storm in Fremont Canyon in February 1854 and brought them to Parowan to recover.

Continue on Main Street one block past the UT 143 turnoff to Old Highway 91. At the turn to the southwest, visit the city park on left (37°50'10.7"N 112°49'42.2"W) to read the historic signs and monuments. Several of the markers are devoted to the Old Spanish Trail.

*N-17: Enoch/Summit Old Spanish Trail Markers*
 Leave the Parowan City Park and head toward Summit, continuing on Old Highway 91. The markers along the trail in this area were installed in the 1950s under the leadership of Cedar City historian William R. Palmer. There is a marker located on the east side of the Mormon Church in Summit (37°48'04.3"N 112°56'04.3"W). It is one of three that remain in this area. The signs display Mexican traders with Indian slaves on horseback. From Summit, cross I-15 and continue south along Old Highway 91 to Enoch. The highway closely follows the trail all the way from Parowan to Enoch.

In Enoch, turn west onto Midvalley Road (37°45'53.2"N 113°01'04.1"W) and drive west .4 miles to Enoch Road, then drive north on this street to 5270 N. Enoch Road, an old church located on the right, now a private residence. Notice the arrow-crowned trail marker. Across the street at 5363 N. Enoch Road is another of the 1950 Palmer markers.

*Arrow-crowned trail marker*

On the street to the left side of this marker, drive west on Jones Lane for .5 miles to the Johnson Fort historic sign (37°46'19.7"N 113°01'55.5"W). The home to the north is on private property and is located on the old

*Johnson Fort historic sign*

fort site. A spring on the property was an important stopping point for Spanish Trail travelers.

After reading the monument, travel east a few feet and turn right onto Tomahawk Road and drive south to Midvalley Road. Turn west (right) (37°45'51.6"N 113°02'36.3"W) on this road and drive to the Enoch City offices, where a sign commemorates the first wagon over the Old Spanish Trail in 1848. The trail was thereafter known as the Southern California Migrant Route.

*N-18: Iron Springs Sites*
        From the Enoch City offices, travel west on Midvalley Road. Note where the road crosses the Lund Highway at 3.5 miles since you will need to return to this point. Drive west an additional 3.4 miles to the Three Peaks Recreation Area. Notice the large BLM/OST sign. Go past the entrance of the recreation area to the gravel road that turns south (37°45'54.9"N 113°10'13.5"W).

The Old Spanish Trail traveled around the south side of the jagged peaks to springs on the west side of the range. Alva Matheson, early Spanish Trail enthusiast, found a number of original trail artifacts next to camping sites by the Three Peaks. The artifacts are in the Museum of the San Rafael in Castle Dale.

Return to the Lund Highway and turn south (right) toward Cedar City. At the highway junction with UT 56, turn west (right) toward

Newcastle. About 1.7 miles west, stop to read the Dominguez-Escalante monument on the right side of the highway, adjacent to the fence of an industrial pipe company.

One mile farther, turn right onto Iron Springs Road and drive 4.8 miles. Past the Iron County Animal Shelter about .3 mile, on the left behind a pair of gates, is an historic sign about the Parley P. Pratt expedition of 1849 (37°44'11.0"N 113°12'58.1"W). Iron Springs is located across the road to the north. The spring was an important stopping place on the Old Spanish Trail.

*Iron Springs sign*

*N-19: Newcastle Trail Sites*

From Iron Springs, the trail went west to Antelope Springs then turned south when it reached the Escalante Desert Valley. Our highway tour will rejoin the trail at Newcastle. Return to UT 56 and head west toward Newcastle. The highway crosses the trail just before it enters Newcastle. The historic sign here on the left just beyond the power lines is perhaps the best example from the 1950 era (37°40'25.1"N 113°32'00.0"W).

*Sign near Newcastle*

Turn left off UT 56 onto the main street of Newcastle. Drive south through town and continue southwest on Bench Road for 5.5 miles. The road follows the Old Spanish Trail closely. Just as the road turns to the west toward Enterprise, there is a large sign for the Jefferson Hunt historic monument.

*Jefferson Hunt monument*

Take the short dirt road on the left to the monument. Hunt traveled the trading trail in 1847 and 1848. He also led the famous Death Valley 49ers to this point in the fall of 1849. Hunt stayed on the Old Spanish Trail and led the wise travelers who stayed with him safely to southern California.

*N-20: Mountain Meadows*

Continue west on Bench Road toward Enterprise. The trail continues south, paralleling the power lines toward the abandoned town of Holt and on to Mountain Meadows. There is always spring water in Holt Canyon. At the junction of Bench Road and UT 18, turn south toward Enterprise. As you enter Enterprise, turn south (left) on UT 18 at Heritage Park (37°34'24.2"N 113°42'16.4"W), and continue toward Mountain Meadows.

About seven miles south of this junction you can view the Mountain Meadows. This area was extremely important for Spanish Trail travelers going both directions. Southbound travelers would spend a week feeding and watering their caravans before they started into the mostly waterless Mojave Desert. John C. Fremont wrote in 1844 that the valley could provide for "a thousand head of horses and cattle."

*Mountain Meadows*

Northbound travelers found the beautiful valley a wonderful reward after a long journey across the southern desert.

Be sure to stop at all four historic sites in the valley. Read about the infamous 1857 massacre which has overshadowed the importance of the place for the Spanish Trail and explains little of the meadow's importance for trail travelers in the early 19th century. The first site, honoring the women and children, is 7.1 miles from Enterprise (37°29'55.9"N 113°37'51.3"W), and the others are a mile or two down the highway.

*N-21: Utah Hill Viewpoint*

The Old Spanish Trail travels south from Mountain Meadows along Magutso Creek, the stream next to the burial site at the Meadows. Return to UT 18 and travel south to Veyo. Turn right onto Gunlock Road. The road intersects Magutso Creek about five miles west of Veyo. The highway overlies the trail south through the community of Gunlock. The Old Spanish Trail leaves Gunlock Road just before its junction with Old Highway 91.

On reaching Old Highway 91, travel west on the historic road that follows the Spanish Trail into Arizona. Armijo traveled on the east side of the mountain.

At Castle Cliff stop to see the challenge of the Mojave Desert ahead. It is the same view that travelers had over 180 years ago. About a mile south of Castle Cliff, Armijo's 1829 path and the Northern Route join.

Follow the old highway to Beaver Dam, Arizona, near Littlefield, Arizona, and the junction of the trail with the Virgin River. Continue on to Mesquite, Nevada, along the path followed by all Spanish Trail travelers. It follows the old highway route along the Virgin River, or you can travel on I-15 to Mesquite, Nevada.

Read the informative Old Spanish Trail sign in front of the Nevada Information Center in Mesquite. The center is located a short distance from the Arizona/Nevada state line.

You have completed your tour of the Northern Route of the Old Spanish Trail through Utah. The route continued on to what is now Los Angeles on a route running south of Las Vegas to Tecopa, Barstow, and San Bernardino, California, before reaching Los Angeles.

*Thank you for traveling the Old Spanish Trail in Arizona and Utah.*

# FOR MORE INFORMATION

www.oldspanishtrail.org
Find us on FaceBook.

www.nps.gov/olsp/index.htm

http://gsenm.org

www.blm.gov/nm/st/en/prog/
recreation/old_spanish_trail.
html

● ● ● ● ● ● ● ● ● ● ● ● ● ● ● ● ●

Passport To Your National Parks

America's natural treasures - our National Parks - are presented in one handy booklet with the Passport To Your National Parks program. This travelogue includes color-coded maps, pre-visit information, illustrations and photographs. It includes a list of every national park area in the United States. Spaces allow you to collect the series of commemorative Passport stamps issued each year.

There are extra pages in the back of the passport book if you want to place all Old Spanish Trail stamps in one location. We suggest that you verify directions and hours of operation to be sure you can get Old Spanish National Historic Trail stamps.

For a complete list of all Old Spanish Trail stamp cancellation locations go to www.nps.gov/olsp/planyourvisit/passport-program. htm.